From Here To There

From Here To There

~

Stepping Stones

by
Jeanne Davis

Illustrated by Pauline Aikman

The C.R. Gibson Company
Norwalk, CT
06856

Preface

A sweet, very ancient love song begins, "I know where I'm goin', and I know who's goin' with me. There's someone I love, and he's the one I'll marry..."

This book takes assorted looks at "Where I'm goin'" — all of us — going from *here* to *there* — and the stepping stones that can lead us to our destination.

Concepts of destination are as varied as individual experiences on this journey that is life; they are as many in number as the travelers — past, present and to come.

Belief is strong among spiritual thinkers that most of us have at least an inkling of "where" we are going and also who the "Someone" we love might be. Most of us cast about to give form and words to our vague, but instinctive perceptions. A few blessed ones through all of time seem always to have had a clear view of the journey — the *from-whence-we-come*, and the *to-where-we-go*; the who, what and where of God, man, the universe and time. The universal mark of these spiritually evolved ones is their utter faith and trust in their Creator and a divine scheme of things. And, they are without fear.

I believe we find the "Someone" by opening up our powers to believe in the availability of a successful journey via the guidance of the Holy Spirit.

"Marry?" The word aptly fits the union of earthly lovers. For the seeking and finding of Love in the spiritual sense, the precise word — the only word — is reunion. Perhaps as you walk the stepping stones of this journey we all share, you will agree.

Jeanne Davis

I choose the way of holy knowing,
the road that goes to wholly being;
my slightest gain forever growing
before the eye of God's all-seeing.
Wholly holy is the goal.

I choose the path of seeker questing,
and trust the road wherever wending
to take me to a place of resting,
all needs met by grace, all doubt ending.
Heart of hearts, Thou art my heart.

J.D.

Getting There

Life in all its guises presents the glorious task of our getting from *here to there*. You may be certain that each step taken on the journey, from start to accomplishment, is a step nearer the strength to continue and the joy-giving realization that we do not travel alone, nor do we travel unassisted or poorly equipped.

While we have uncertainties and fear of the journey we undertake with the first breath of life, somehow, very deep down, "We feel that we are greater than we know," as Wordsworth put it. Trust that feeling! It is but one of many gifts of divine grace that come with the chief gift, life itself.

Love, Light, Power, Strength, Wisdom created you. They keep you, from everlasting to everlasting. That which holds bird, cloud, sun, moon, stars and planets aloft is able to — willing to — hold you up. Each step on the road, be it on the journey of daily routine, or mental undertaking, or a facing up to trial and challenge, becomes an entry in your track record book. Each time your invisible muscles carry you forward and upward, they, like their physical counterparts, grow in strength, serviceability and dependability.

The great journey, the spiritual one that began in the mind of your Creator, leads to reunion with the Creator, the source of all. This is a journey to enlightenment and altogether whole Being. Nothing less than a return to God and the "ingredients" that made you, is where you are headed.

As rivers have their source in some far off fountain,
so the human spirit has its source. To find this
fountain of spirit is to learn the secret of heaven
and earth.

LAO-TZU

God is the friend of silence. Trees, flowers, grass
grow in silence. See the stars, moon and sun, how
they move in silence.

MOTHER TERESA

We do not understand but somehow we are part of
a creative destiny reaching backward and forward to
infinity...In us is the longing for unity. We are
impelled by a hidden instinct to reunion with the
parts of the larger heart of the universe.

JOHN ELOF BOODIN

This deep desire...being one with the universe...and
with God...that is what we wish for most, whether
we know it or not.

FRITZ KUNKEL

Company Along the Way

*An agreeable companion on a journey is as good as
a carriage.*

PUBLILIUS SYRUS

We are never alone. Side-by-side we — you, me, the Creator of
all, and those who share the inspiring, informing insights and
discoveries of their journey — all guide each other, help each
other on the road. The entire distance.

Among agreeable and excellent companions are assuredly
an open mind and heart; an eagerness to be of help to ourselves
and others, but also a willingness to accept assistance from others and, of course, utter trust in the company of the Creator.

Have we the stamina, the courage and wisdom to take the mini-
journeys each day presents and — the hardest of them all —
the spiritual pilgrimage to the recognition and acceptance of
the Creator's continued provision, support and love? The
divine abundance that sets us free from every kind of fear? Do
we have what it takes to not be overwhelmed by the supposed
hazards of the road? We have.

Addressing the Canadian Senate and House of Commons
in Ottawa during the soul-wrenching days of World War II,

a time when everyone was called upon to give the best effort possible for survival and ultimate success in the war's conclusion, *Winston Churchill* growled in his inimitable Olympian voice: "We have not journeyed all this way across the centuries, across the oceans, across the mountains, across the prairies, because we are made of sugar candy." Nor have we journeyed from the Creator's first touch to this very day "because we are made of sugar candy." No. We are the *stuff* of our Creator, in whose image and likeness we were made.

In *choosing* to reflect the power and glory of the Creator rather than settle for the limitations of man's idea of man, we do take on the image and likeness of our Maker. In *choosing* to accept our status as children of God, we consent to being heirs to all that is divine.

God's child, or man's? The choice is ours and it is the very substance of the road we take.

There was a woman of our time who understood the divine connection and never doubted its miraculous meeting of her needs. She was known as Peace Pilgrim and for twenty-eight years she walked the length and breadth of the United States with nothing but the clothes on her back and a few personal necessities in her pockets. She utterly simplified her life to travel in behalf of her message: peace...inner, outer, and universal.

She said of herself, "...I wear a lettered tunic — it says 'Peace Pilgrim' on the front. I feel that is my name now — it emphasizes my mission instead of me. And on the back it says '25,000 miles on foot for peace.' ...I have said I will walk until given shelter and fast until given food, remaining a wanderer until mankind has learned the way of peace. And I can truthfully tell you that without ever asking for anything, I have been supplied with everything needed for my journey…"

Peace Pilgrim demonstrates dramatically the truth of… "faith being the substance of things hoped for, the evidence of things not seen." *Hebrews 5:12*

Over the years this remarkable traveler's hair grew white. Her serene face continued to give heart to those she met, and her faith continued to bring into manifestation all that she required each day of her pilgrimage. Her earthly journey ended peacefully on a rural road in Indiana in 1981. Her brave example of faith is a shining example of the divine connection between Peace Pilgrim and her Creator, and, it follows, between you and yours.

While each of us makes the journey that is life quite in our own way and at our own pace, stepping stones on the path — such as Peace Pilgrim's witness to God's ever-present provision — mark the way for those who will be guided.

A lack of personal experience of healing or deliverance should not be taken as proof that these attainments are impossible. Trust. There are solutions and ideas, corrections and overcomings of such magnitude and variety as to defy mere mortal imagination. These divinely designed experiences are available to the degree that we are available to trust and believe in their reality.

As we open our eyes in the morning let us at once open our minds, hearts and souls to the lavish bounty that is our birthright. Let us open our entire being to the always available good within the seeker's reach. The Christian admonition to "Be still and know that I am God," ranks among the most instructive of stepping stones guiding the traveler.

A very old, but still widely used Quaker expression is "Way will open." Way will open to solving a problem, to being restored to health, or peace of mind, financial security, or to being pointed in a right direction. However, way opens only to the degree that we stand aside and consent to its doing so.

God respects me when I work, but he loves me
when I sing.

RABINDRANATH TAGORE

For there is strength in you greater than any
strength of your own, the Will that stirs within you
when your own will is at rest.

GREGORY VLASTOS

Wisdom and growth insist on an openness to differences of all sorts. Your companions on the journey may speak in a language not yours. Signposts may appear in a strange mode. Within frames of reference that are not yours… in attire unlike yours, in times and spaces and places that are not yours…can abide perfect fulfillment of every need for the journey. Watch and listen.

> *Legend has it that Tobias, the young hero of the Apocryphal Book of Tobit, sent by his blind father to conduct business in a distant city, was accompanied on his journey by the angel Raphael, disguised as a fellow traveler. Under guidance of Raphael, Tobias safely completed his mission, triumphed over a demon, acquired a wife and returned to cure his father's blindness.*
>
> PATRICIA FAILING

While the story of Tobias and his journey with the Archangel Raphael has all the elements of myth, melodrama even borderline satire, its message remains, nonetheless, the important one of attentiveness to our companions as we travel from here to there. If we allow them to make their presence known to us, there is always the God-given possibility of fresh, useful information being freely given to us.

> *Be not forgetful to entertain strangers, for thereby some have entertained angels unawares.*
>
> HEBREWS 13:2

> *…However much any one of us may know of God, there will always be unexplored fields in the realms of expression.*
>
> H. EMILIE CADY

En Route to Reality

Is there, in truth, a *there* where we long to be? According to the scriptures of all major and minor religions including the spoken religious texts of tribal peoples the world over — the answer is a resounding yes! In our core we can echo the yes.

> *When you are halfway there, you stop disbelieving in there.*
>
> HUGH PRATHER

> *I do dimly perceive that whilst everything around me is ever-changing, ever-dying, there is underlying all that changes a Living Power that is changeless, that holds all together, that creates, dissolves, and recreates.*
>
> MAHATMA GANDHI

> *All I ask is the heaven above — and the road below me.*
>
> ROBERT LOUIS STEVENSON

All known existence points beyond itself.

REINHOLD NIEBUHR

There is Reality as well as a state of spiritually understanding Reality. There is both the journey and the goal. The journey and the journeyer are one in objective—to get from a *here* to a *there*.

"All is one," say the religions and theosophies of the East.

"I and the Father are one," Jesus declared. It is significant that in prayer He addressed "Our" Father, not "My" Father, demonstrating His comforting insistence on our being joint heirs with Him to the Father's powers. With our brother Jesus, we share the lessons of the road—to heal, to think rightly, to be unafraid, to bring deliverance.

Atonement with our world, ourselves and our fellows is a healing and adjusting of all that is our essential Being. Atonement gives comfort…we aren't alone in *at-one-ment*; we aren't alienated or separated—in *at-one-ment* we are there spiritually and actually.

The gift of grace is one of the keys to the journey. The gift of spiritual awakening, of coming to comprehend the vast aspect and dimensions to Reality may be the greatest of them all. In our material life, time and space are defined by a limited, earthly view. Yet in the very center of our Being there is the unshakable certainty that there is infinitely more to what is than meets the eye. Discovering and utilizing it all is what the journey is all about. It is accepting as our right all that Deity made, not just for us but for all of creation.

In learning to find our own Center of Being through being silent and listening, through meditation on the magnificence of life and living, through practicing the ways of the Holy Spirit… through prayer, through behaving bravely and trustingly… through all of this, we find not only our Center but the realization that it expands to include all space and time and all Reality.

> …we are spirits, not animals, and…something
> is going on in space and time and beyond space
> and time.

WINSTON CHURCHILL

I choose to be here now, and for what time brings
of all that's yet to be.
What was and is, is all eternity
within whose space creation sings,
the voice of Being rings.

I choose to share present laughter, present tears,
to freely and gayly spend my given years
in fond trust of God's coin in goodly store,
enough for evermore.

Today I see all the world as glory;
today I see all that is life's story
as quickening of the soul's brightest dream
and, yes, the working of God's perfect scheme.

J.D.

Be
Present

*If it took You two billion years to bring me here, help
me to be all here — as You are.*

ALLAN HUNTER

"Help me to be all here…" At-one-ment and the perfecting of the soul notwithstanding, it behooves us to do and show and share as much enlightenment as we have now. In so presenting the degree of spiritual enrichment for the benefit of our own welfare and that of all in occupation of Planet Earth with us now, we strengthen and expand, nurture and encourage the further unfolding of cosmic truths.

Be fully present at each stage of your journey. Be present for all whom you meet, for the scenery along the way, for the beauty and the harshness, the joy and sorrow. Be there for the triumphs and relish them with uninhibited joy — even cheers! Be there for your own humanity, including frailty, and that of fellow travelers.

*Behold how good and how pleasant it is for
brethren to dwell together in unity!*

PSALM 133:1

*Wisely improve the present. It is thine…Go forth to
meet the Future, without fear and with a manly heart.*

HENRY WADSWORTH LONGFELLOW

For he lives twice who can at once employ
The present well, and ev'n the past enjoy.

ALEXANDER POPE

With due respect to time — both the mysterious everlasting and that contrived by man — we do ourselves a great favor in giving the day-to-day of life the same concentration and courtship we, as spiritual travelers, give to the great journey.

Now is the accepted time.

II CORINTHIANS 6:2

Each "now" accorded the best we have in understanding and generosity of heart and spirit, becomes a part of our entirety, the sum of our parts in wholeness — everything you desire and need.

Act, act in the living present! Heart within, and God
O'er head!

HENRY WADSWORTH LONGFELLOW

God is God of the present moment. Just as you are he
finds you, receives you and takes you, not just as you
were but as you are at this moment.

MEISTER ECKHART

Pay attention to the aspect of life that is now, rather than let it slip by unattended to in favor of speculation on the "then" to come. No time aspect of living has need to take precedence over any other; each stage is crucial to the divine fulfillment of all.

> ...To be present is to be vulnerable, to be able to be hurt, to be willing to be spent — but it is also to be awake, alive, and engaged actively in the immediate assignment that has been laid upon us...there is no task God has called us to...that is more challenging than being made inwardly ready to be present where we are.

DOUGLAS STEERE

We are Free to be Happy

Happiness on the road is not only permissible, it is, from all quarters, encouraged.

> *Gladness of the heart is the life of man, and the joyfulness of a man prolongeth his days…Look upon the rainbow and praise Him that made it.*
>
> THE APOCRYPHA

> *Praise ye the Lord…Praise him for his mighty acts: praise him according to his excellent greatness. Praise him with the sound of trumpet…Praise him with timbrel and dance: praise him with stringed instruments and organs…Praise him upon the high sounding cymbals. Let everything that hath breath praise the Lord.*
>
> PSALM 150:1-6

Yes, skipping cheerfully down the road is one more delight of the trip and, like laughter, it's good for you.

The gift of gaiety may itself be the greatest good fortune, and the most serious step toward maturity.

IRWIN EDMAN

It is comely fashion to be glad — joy is the grace we say to God.

JEAN INGELOW

To be joyful, then, is to give thanks. And why not? Christians, indeed, are taught, "The Lord loveth a cheerful giver."

Happiness is a present attitude…not a future consideration.

HUGH PRATHER

The Grace of Possibility

*...we are surrounded by possibilities that are
infinite, and the purpose of human life is to grasp as
much as we can out of that infinitude.*

ALFRED NORTH WHITEHEAD

The possibilities for grasping more of infinite truth, exist along-side the possibilities presented for our well-being here on Earth. It appears to be fact that all possibilities are kindred in make-up — that is, they take the form of opportunity to take on a project, sought or unsought. And, in so doing we become evermore aware of the possibility within our immediate reach.

*What I mean by the Muse is that unimpeded clear-ness of intuitive powers...Should these faculties
have free play, I believe they will open new, deeper
and purer sources of joyous inspiration than have
yet refreshed the earth.*

MARGARET FULLER

Margaret Fuller brings into relation with possibility much of what has been given expression before in this book: power, intuition, openings into "deep" and "pure sources," and, oh, the enlivening word, *refreshment!*

In a 1963 speech John F. Kennedy pointed out to his listeners, "When written in Chinese, the word *crisis* is composed of two characters. One represents danger and the other represents opportunity." Is that not "possibility" at every turn? Imagination is the great friend of possibility.

Imagination is more important than knowledge.

EINSTEIN

But as it is written, Eye hath not seen, nor ear heard, neither have entered into the heart of man, the things which God has prepared for them that love Him.

I CORINTHIANS 2:9

Problems are only opportunities in work clothes.

HENRY J. KAISER

For the vast majority of us the journey from here to there involves work as well as faith, hope, trust, and the insights born of prayer and meditation — not forgetting the insights born of experience and living. There are those who have withdrawn from the world and found enlightenment in solitude and a life of meditation only. And there are those who take the steps down the road in work clothes, which in high moments of spiritual openings can take on the lightness and uplift of wings!

Joy, possibility, opportunity, growing and knowing; God, man and the universe — thee and me, we give and we take, we share and we lift up, having chosen to give the journey our total attention. Rightly so!

All are but parts of one stupendous whole, Whose body nature is, and God the soul.

ALEXANDER POPE

Be Not Afraid

What, or who, is our enemy? Is it a nation, a person or an idea so different to our own that it is intolerable and thus to be loathed? Is our enemy real, or only in our perception of some challenge or threat?

As we would succeed in our journey and as we would also be joyfully present on Earth, let us claim fearlessness as a working part of our ongoing. "Perfect love casteth out fear." *I John 4:18*

Love in some form and degree is the miraculous word in ridding ourselves of fear and enemies. Love is a journey within the great journey and it, as we are all aware, is the hardest one.

Learning by rote is not the ideal method, but sometimes it is a good starting place; sometimes it gives us a focus for concentration just as the hands in the steeple of prayer draw the mind and soul to the purpose before us.

There is a story about the theater that informs as fully as it entertains. I pass it along as an analogy to the spiritual exercises that lead us to a coming to know.

Night after night in one scene of the drama, an actor was fired at by the villain of the piece and, clutching his chest he would cry out, "My God! I've been shot." One night the villain, who suspected the actor of trying to steal his wife in real life, put a real bullet in the pistol and fired point blank. As always the actor grabbed at his chest and started to fall. But this time he had a look of genuine surprise on his face as he shouted, "My God! I *have* been shot!"

Even if you can not now fully believe the following affirmation, say it repeatedly and thoughtfully. You may be happily surprised one day to realize, "My God! I and Love are one!"

God is Love. I know I was born with the ability to love. I and Love, with or without consent, are one. I pray to leave off blocking Love's effort to work for good through me. To love is to give one's best and to try one's best to be the evolved and enlightened soul that is our destiny.

Love for that which we perceive as unlovable is not easily achieved, but it is possible. It is to our best personal interests to put forth every effort in behalf of peaceable coexistence. This can be looked on as spade work for actually touching our supposed enemy in a manner beneficial to both.

Not-loving, like fear, has an unpleasant way of making a scapegoat of one's body. Hating and fearing can churn up even chemical reactions that make us physically and emotionally ill. An excellent exercise in spiritual development and spiritual fitness is to actually make a list of what you and your "enemy" — fear, threat, person or whatever — share in common. Where do you meet? What joins you as opposed to what separates you? Such lists are supremely difficult to make but they can work magic in setting wrongs to rights.

As we let go of fear and unloving feelings, we free-up our other abilities, to work toward a coming to realize the Creator's gifts. We see the possibilities and opportunities that are ever present to keep us safe.

The eternal God is thy refuge, and underneath are
the everlasting arms...He shall thrust out the enemy...

DEUT. 33:27

The instances of delivery from impossible circumstances are numerous enough to make us reconsider the word "impossible": earthquake victims buried alive for days and surviving to be rescued...campers ringed in by a raging forest fire finding a way out, where none had appeared to exist before...fishermen in a floundering boat, having gone weeks with only rain water to drink and a few crackers to dole out, conducting a religious service for themselves and the death that appeared but hours away, only to be spotted and saved by another fishing boat — it, too, in the middle of the Pacific Ocean, far from its regular course. William Wordsworth wrote in a child's album, "The daisy, by the shadow that it casts, protects the lingering dewdrop from the sun." Can our protection by the Creator of the daisy be any less?

The Lord my pasture shall prepare,
And feed me with a shepherd's care;
His presence shall my wants supply,
And guard me with a watchful eye:
My noonday walks He shall attend,
And all my midnight hours defend.

CHRISTIAN HYMNAL

All in an instant the size of a drop
the rain has released the resin sachet
of a scrap wood hut secure in a tree,
smelling of childhood's bewitching bouquet.
It was there in the musk, mysterious air
— locked safely away by some fairy key —
a girl, a doll and a calico cat
hid high and dry in a house in a tree.
Sealed in forever the damp scent of wood
is the sweet secret of balsam and clay —
the essence of earth, of moldering leaves —
the magic aroma of rainy day play.
Forever, remembering rain wetted wood
conjures a tree with a house at the top,
where perfume was made in a long ago rain
all in an instant the size of a drop.

J.D.

To Have
and
To Hold

The Grace of Memory

Memory, remembrance, recollection — or *re*-collection meaning to gather together again — are crucially linked to our journey from here to there — to enlightenment, to spiritual understanding. Progress can be advanced in the simple recollection of previous steps well-taken, remembrance of the joy and uplift that crowned the achievement.

Memory enriches the present with all its visions of those dear to us, scenes dear to us, experiences so wonderful we never wish to let them go. No need. The blessing of memory makes possible having and holding, cherishing and enjoying all that has gone before. Memory binds all to our hearts and souls forever. Memory of successful effort on the journey gives added strength and confidence to present tries.

> *Remembered joys are never past;*
> *At once the fountain, stream and sea,*
> *they were, they are, they shall be.*

JAMES MONTGOMERY

> *… but, it does me good to sing in childish key,*
> *that which was set to music long ago.*

CLO M. BETTES

J. Robert Oppenheim observed that aspects of discoveries in atomic physics were not *wholly unfamiliar.*

Carl Jung, the analyst/philosopher, talked of "primordial images, archaic remnants…part of the past, part of our memory pattern."

> *…that odd state of mind wherein we fitfully and testingly remember some previous scene or incident, of which the one now passing appears to be but the echo and reduplication.*
>
> NATHANIEL HAWTHORNE

> *It's a poor sort of memory that only works backwards.*
>
> LEWIS CARROLL

It may be that memory is a divinely bestowed gift designed to keep fresh the joy of past day-to-day human experiences as well as the lessons learned. It may be as well that memory is a compass to use on the journey that links us to the Source from which we come. And, since the journey takes us to that Source, memory may also be available to us *before* an experience that is to come.

What we call instinct, intuition, insight or clever deduction, may indeed be memory — memory of all that has gone before.

Certainly in the physical evolution of all Creation, vestiges of that which was before remain: the glorious feathers adorning one species of our dearest companions are remnants of the scales of when once they were serpents. What a distance *those* pilgrims journeyed!

Who is to say precisely how far we have come and how far we have yet to go? Neither spiritual nor physical evolution seems to have run their course. Moths that live in certain trees in a

London park have, within a few moth generations, changed their coloration to match trees discolored by air pollution.

If physical evolution can be as dramatic as serpent to bird, can there be a limit to how evolved a soul can become? There is always tomorrow and the particulars of tomorrow. Tomorrow, like now and was, simply is.

Blessedly, our road from here to there is adorned with happiness, health and love, abundance and growth. Companionship. The demands of the journey, the tests of endurance, form the muscles of physical and spiritual fitness. Each new day, like each new thought, carries with it memories of other days and other thoughts — helps for present needs. Because we have exercised those muscles, they toughen, form, and grow even more reliable.

> *Our birth is but a sleep and a forgetting:*
> *The soul that rises with us, our life's Star,*
> *Hath had elsewhere its setting,*
> *And cometh from afar.*
> *Not in entire forgetfulness and not in utter nakedness,*
> *But trailing clouds of glory do we come*
> *From God, who is our home.*

WILLIAM WORDSWORTH

To Love God is to Love All

Be kind to yourself. When you heed the Biblical advice to "Love thy neighbor as thyself," you may correctly infer that we are supposed to love ourselves. The genuine sense of self-worth, of course, has nothing to do with self-aggrandizement, strutting and puffing, but has to do with God's man, the one who came equipped with the possibility of becoming God-like. God-like. I mean the caring, loving, helpful, unselfish, kind, gentle, forgiving, powerful, Holy and magnificent aspect of the Deity in whose image He made us.

The love we give our neighbor is an acknowledgement of our being of the same species. If we don't love our own kind… brothers…and sisters…who can we, then, love?

Are we less loving than the elephants who form a protective circle around members of their kind who are giving birth? Are we less sensitive than a community of chimpanzees, who observe the entrance of a widow into their midst with guarded hospitality? She has watched this community for days. Now she enters into their ground, demurely…even fearfully. Will they take her in or leave her to wander the forest alone and bereft? She walks bravely around the inside of the circle and puts her hand out to each individual eyeing her. After thoughtful consideration each, one by one, accepts the offer of her hand. She has been taken in. She has a home. She has companions to share the journey.

"Love thy neighbor as thyself." Love your neighbor as though he were you.

In his never-ceasing practice of the presence of God, the saintly Brother Lawrence fully understood the need to be kind to oneself, the need to be patient.

> …*when he failed in his duty he simply confessed his*
> *fault, saying to God, 'I shall never do otherwise, if*
> *Thou leavest me to myself'…after this he gave*
> *himself no further uneasiness about it…*
>
> DE BEAUFORT

> *Gird on thy sword, O man, thy strength endue,*
> *In fair desire thine earth-born joy renew.*
> *Live thou thy life beneath the making sun*
> *Till beauty, Truth, and Love in thee are one.*
>
> ROBERT BRIDGES

Love all God's creation, the whole and every grain of sand in it. Love every leaf, every ray of God's light. Love the animals, love the plants, love everything. If you love everything, you will perceive the divine mystery in things. Once you perceive it, you will begin to comprehend it better every day. And you will come at last to love the whole world with an all-embracing love.

DOSTOYEVSKY

There are trembling ones who dwell in fear
Within the cell of some terror's wall;
There are those like moons that shine afar,
In the wait for their dark to fall;
There are singular souls who find a way
Where none has ever trod —
I? I trust being in the here and now
And leave the how to God.

Thus, from my house here by the side of now's road,
With how aching to make itself known
In ways I can only sense to be right —
I'm glad in good time to be shown.
For I am remade, as in a season's return,
Faith mulching my soil, turning sod.
And — acting out thanks for each here and now —
I trust details to God.

J.D.

The House We Live in

The house we live in now is just the physical body, the material universe, the very Earth that is our lovely planet. Wondrously miraculous, beautiful, phenomenal, mysterious and intricate as this vast physicality is, it is but the visible and tangible aspect of the spiritual home that is *of* God and *is* God. Physicality is as legitimate to our makeup as is spirituality, soulfulness. It is a part of the whole and should not be denigrated. But a house is not necessarily a home.

It takes a heap o'livin' in a house t'make it home…

EDGAR A. GUEST

The universe begins to look more like a great thought than a great machine.

SIR JAMES JEANS

All are but parts of one stupendous whole,
Whose body nature is, and God the soul.

ALEXANDER POPE

Home, then, is where we are heading…the *there* where all is safe, realized and fulfilled. Home is where we become complete.

Hidden deep in the heart of things,
Thou carest for growth and life.
The seed becomes shoot, the bud a blossom,
The flower becomes fruit.

RABINDRANATH TAGORE

To be what we are, and to become what we are
capable of becoming is the only goal of life.

ROBERT LOUIS STEVENSON

God by Any Other Name

What truth the teenaged Juliet speaks when she cries out to her beloved Romeo, "What's in a name? That which we call a rose by any other name would smell as sweet." By what name God is addressed is not important. Deity is, was, always shall be, and may be praised by whichever name or title is at the time appropriate to the worshiper.

My God is always obliging and available. At times of insecurity and anxiety when I tremble with the uncertainty of a child, there is my beloved Father to turn to. In the darkness of fear, my Mother's protective breast and murmured sounds of reassurance soothe and comfort.

In times of intellectual activity within my interior life, God is Law, unfailing Principle. My metaphysical being finds both comfort and guidance in Divine Mind, Perfect (healing) Love, the miraculous Holy Spirit that when called up in utter trust, adjusts and corrects all that is "wrong." Sometimes Deity is The Force, Omnipotent Energy, Core of My Center. By whatever name and in whichever aspect approached, my God is there as eternal Power and Glory, the All in All.

On foot, aboard a ship or jetliner…in a strange or threatening, or inhospitable place, where I am, so is God!

The mystical reunion with The Source takes place when called upon. And that, finally, is prayer. If nothing else in our journey…with all its twists, turns, struggles upward, falling downward…with it all, as we pray we learn to pray. Ultimately we communicate with The Source.

> *Prayer is not asking for things — not even for the best things; it is going where they are.*
>
> GERALD HEARD

This then, is the phenomenon that fills deserts with manna, and feeds the hungry with loaves and fishes. It is the phenomenon that provides vessels of endless wine and raises the crippled from the beds they take up and walk with. It is *even* the phenomenon that brings the mountain to Mohammed.

To know that this fulfillment exists even before asked for is one of the most powerful truths the mysteries offer. As the heart is reaching out, the Divine Heart is coming to meet it. Claim it!

Our journey, then, to there brings us to our Creator. We may relax in our striving, we may quit trying hard — we may safely "Let go and Let God". God, by whatever name, IS. The great spiritual favor we can do for ourselves is to be very, very still and to quietly, happily know just that.

The wild geese do not intend to cast their reflections,
the water has no mind to receive their image...

ZEN PROVERB

As we consent to the way that opens before us, it does. We have our task and God has His. It is not our place to instruct God in the how of doing it.

Godspeed

Our journey, then, is of the soul and body, mind and heart, and of the spirit. Its goal is *re-union* and *at-one-ment* with our Creator. Perhaps that reunion is the coming into possession of one's own soul.

Our journey makes significant stops by the roadside to observe, learn, assimilate and evaluate. We stop and smell the roses along the way and view the scenery in all directions. The experience of the journey itself and what it takes to get from *here* to *there* is the very key to the Kingdom.

John Buchan (Lord Tweedsmuir) was born and grew up in the beautiful border country of Scotland and England. From earliest childhood his great love was fishing and his greatest joy — his growing sense of nature and God as related in spirit — was encouraged by his time spent in glen and wood, and by streams in the highlands and lowlands. In his book *Pilgrim's Way* he remembers this childhood. His observation was keen, his sense of Holy Presence profound.

Here he speaks of a mystical behavior in a so-called lower form of life:

> *...I noticed then something which I have often since observed, that there was a short spell just before the*

dark when no fish would take…there would come a
time when there seemed to be a sudden hush in the
world, when 'nature was breathless with adoration'
and the trout had halted to reflect on their sins.
When that hour came I would lay down my rod until
the flop of a rising fish told me that the wheels of the
world were going round again…the humble and
pious trout…

JOHN BUCHAN

Can not we pause at least once a day in breathless adoration as does the pious trout? A daily turning inward is a refreshing and nourishing pause in our journey.

On opening your eyes in the morning, pause to open your spirit to the presence of the Creator. Give thanks for another day of the journey. Pause to send a thought of love, or healing, or comfort, to someone in need. Ask to be shown, in this new day, how God's work might be in need of your particular attention. Pray. Travel happily and with trust.

And though the ground was rough and I was over
taken by fierce storms, I did not turn back; for when
the soul is once started on the soul's journey, it can
never turn back…Can you the [questing] pilgrim
now go on with your old life as if nothing happened?
The whole universe has happened…

ANONYMOUS

Acknowledgments

The editor and the publisher have made every effort to trace the ownership of all copyrighted material and to secure permission from copyright holders of such material. In the event of any question arising as to the use of any material the publisher and the editor, while expressing regret for inadvertent error, will be pleased to make the necessary corrections in future printings. Thanks are due to the following authors, publishers, publications and agents for permission to use the material indicated.

A. P. WATT LTD., on behalf of the Ron Lord Tweedsmuir of Elsfield, CBE, for an excerpt from *Pilgrim's Way* by John Buchan. (Originally published by Houghton-Mifflin, 1940.)

QUAKER HOME SERVICE, Friends House, London NE1 2BJ, for an excerpt from *God is Silence* by Pierre Lacout. (First published in English by Friends Home Service Committee in 1970 and reprinted by FHS in 1973 and 1978.)

HARPER & ROW, for an excerpt from *The Choice is Always Ours*, co-editors Dorothy Berkley Phillips, Elizabeth Boyden Howes and Lucille M. Nixon, by Fritz Kunkel; for an excerpt from *The Divine Milieu* by Pierre Teilhard de Chardin (1960 edition).

SCRIBNER EDUCATIONAL PUBLISHERS, for an excerpt from *Discerning the Signs of the Times* by Reinhold Niebuhr (originally published by Charles Scribner & Sons).

ALFRED A. KNOPF, INC., for an excerpt from *Markings* by Dag Hammarskjold, translated by Leif Sjoberg and W.H. Auden.

HANUMAN FOUNDATION, for an excerpt from *Be Here Now* by Ram Dass.

UNITY SCHOOL OF CHRISTIANITY, for an excerpt from *Lessons in Truth* by H. Emilie Cady.

FRIENDS OF PEACE PILGRIM, 43480, Cedar Avenue, Hemet, CA 92344, for an excerpt from *Steps Toward Inner Peace*, by Peace Pilgrim. (Permission to quote not required, but address given for readers interested in tapes, other writings by and about Peace Pilgrim).

Also acknowledged sources:

JOHN ELOF BOODIN, Copyright 1925, for his *Cosmic Evolution*, of which an excerpt is used in this volume.

REAL PEOPLE PRESS, 1970 publishers of *Notes to Myself* by Hugh Prather.

CLARKSON N. POTTER, INC., 1983 publishers of *Best-Loved Art from American Museums*, by Patricia Failing.

PENDLE HILL PUBLICATIONS, Wallingford, PA 19086, Pamphlet #151, *On Being Present Where You Are* by Douglas Steere (originally the 1967 James Backhouse Lecture in Tasmania).

THE REV. ALLAN A. HUNTER, personally known to the writer/compiler of this book.

BARTLETT'S FAMILIAR QUOTATIONS, (1955 edition) published by Little Brown & Co.

THE HOLY BIBLE, King James Version and Revised Standard Version.

APOCRYPHA and SEPTUAGINT

ASSORTED NOTES derived from public lectures and newspaper clippings as well as heirloom family papers and books from worldwide sources over many generations. Also, the writer/compiler of this book was for many years an active journalist covering a wide range of assignments and from which come some of the observations presented here.